Jarvis Ontario in Photos, Saving Our History One Photo at a Time

Photography
by Barbara Raué
2013

Series Name:
Cruising Ontario

Book 34: Jarvis

Cover photo: Jones-Doughty Residence – one of the oldest homes in Jarvis, built in 1865 by local builders with the bricks supplied by the local Rodgers Brick Yard. Italianate style with dichromatic brickwork, arched voussoirs with keystones, paired cornice brackets, bay window on side

Series Name: Cruising Ontario

Book 1: London
Book 2: Dundas
Book 3: Hamilton
Book 4: Oakville
Book 5: Chesley
Book 6: Stoney Creek
Book 7: Waterdown
Book 8: Owen Sound
Book 9: Mount Forest
Book 10: Dundalk
Book 11: Burford
Book 12: Waterford
Book 13: Drumbo
Book 14: Sheffield
Book 15: Tavistock
Book 16: Ancaster and Mount Hope
Book 17: Innerkip
Book 18: Brantford
Book 19: Burlington
Book 20: Guelph
Book 21: Ayr
Book 22: Erin
Book 23: Goderich
Book 24: Lucknow
Book 25: Paris
Book 26: Toronto
Book 27: Beaver Valley
Book 28: Collingwood
Book 29: Peterborough
Book 30: Orangeville Beginnings Part 1
Book 31: Orangeville Part 2 and Area
Book 32: Port Elgin
Book 33: Southampton
Book 34: Jarvis

Other Books by Barbara Raue

Coins of Gold

Arrows, Indians and Love

The Life and Times of Barbara
Volume 1: Inventions That Have Enhanced My Life
Volume 2: Entertainment That I Have Enjoyed
Volume 3: East Coast Trips
Volume 4: Olympics Have Always Intrigued Me
Volume 5: Wonders of the World
Volume 6: Caribbean Cruises We Have Enjoyed
Volume 7: Animals
Volume 8: Storms and Other Major Disasters in My Lifetime
Volume 9: Wars, Terrorist Attacks and Major Disasters

The Cromwell Family Book

Visit Barbara's website to view all of her books
http://barbararaue.ericraue.com

Jarvis

Jarvis is located near the towns of Simcoe, Cayuga, Port Dover and Hagersville. Highways 3 and 6 form a crossroads near the centre of the community.

Jarvis has some excellent examples of brick architecture. Many of the historic homes were built after 1873. Most of the town's restaurants and shops are clustered around the intersection of the highways. Most buildings are red brick.

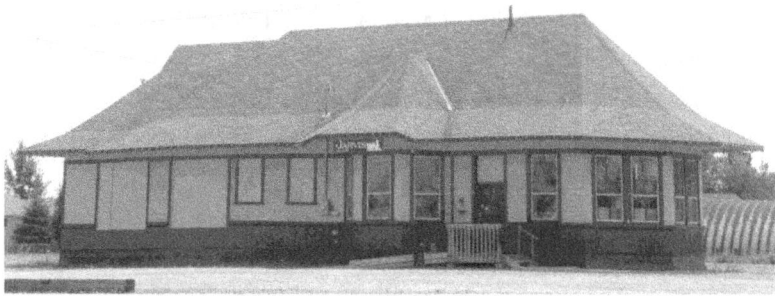

Jarvis Train Station

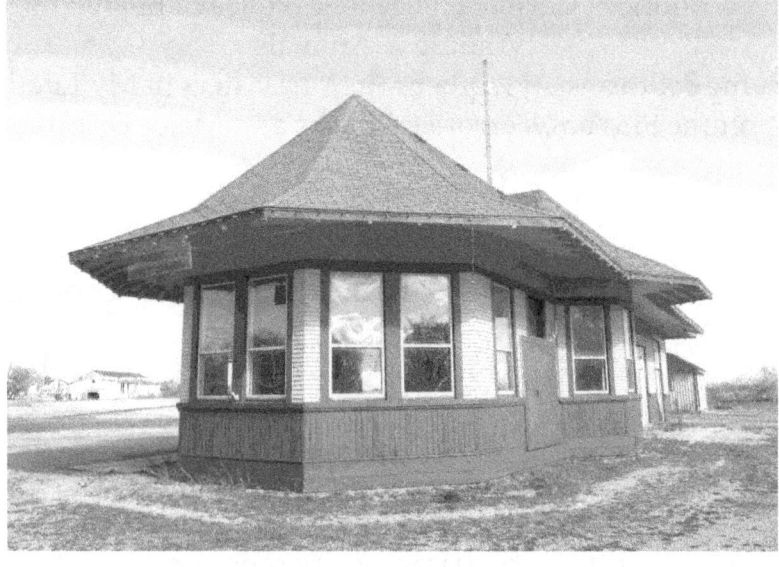

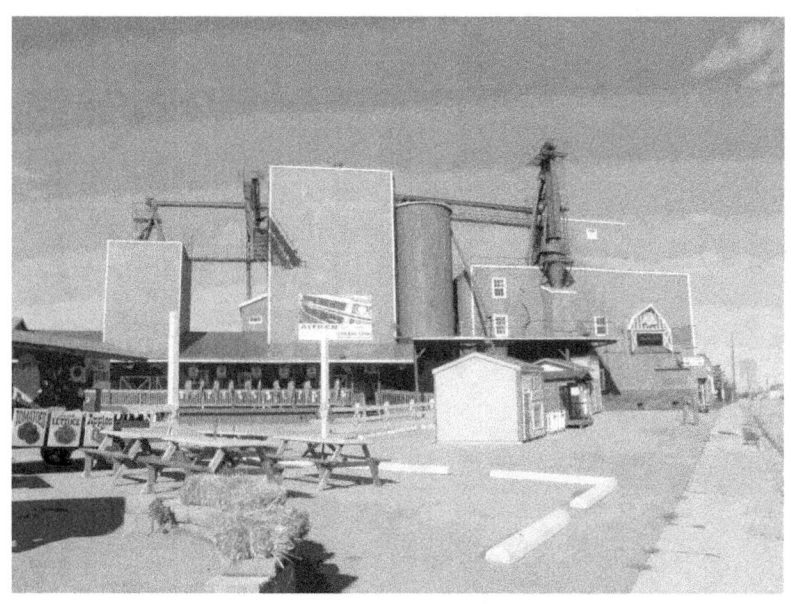

Grain elevators – now an antique market

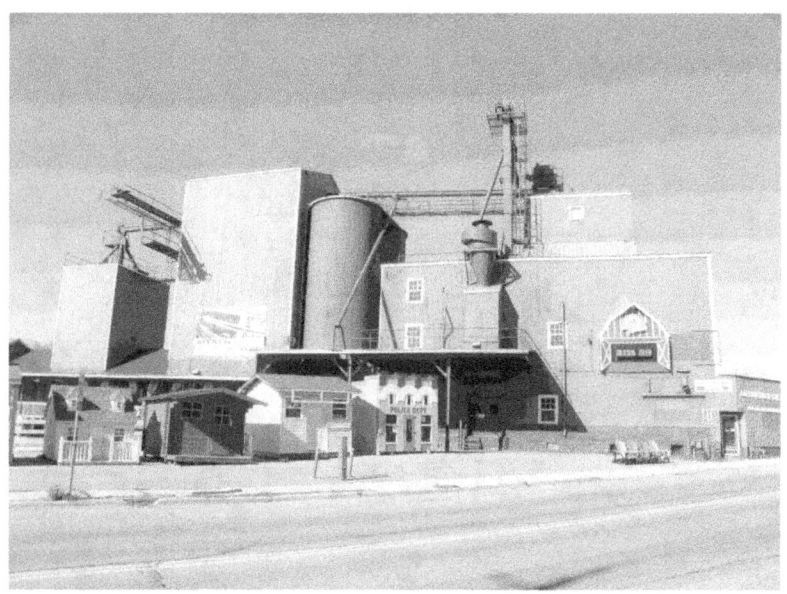

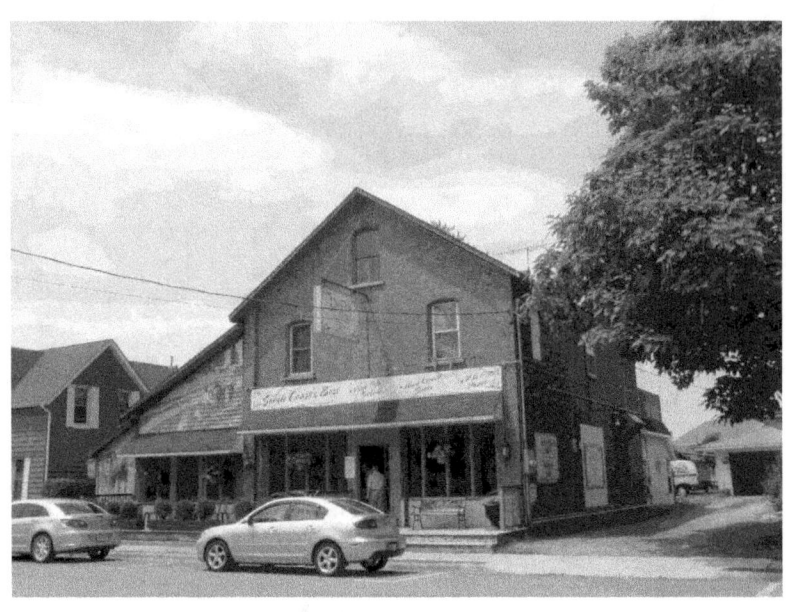

Dina D's Fine Family Dining – a great place for lunch – built in the 1880s

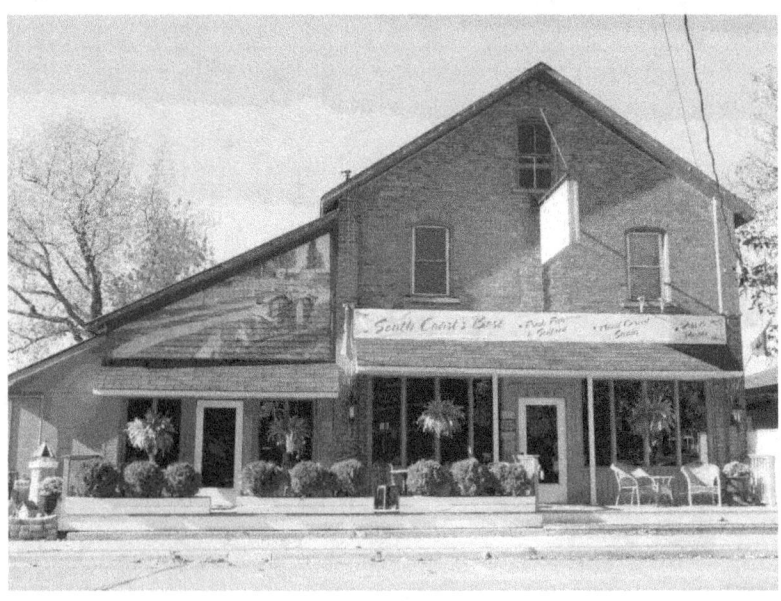

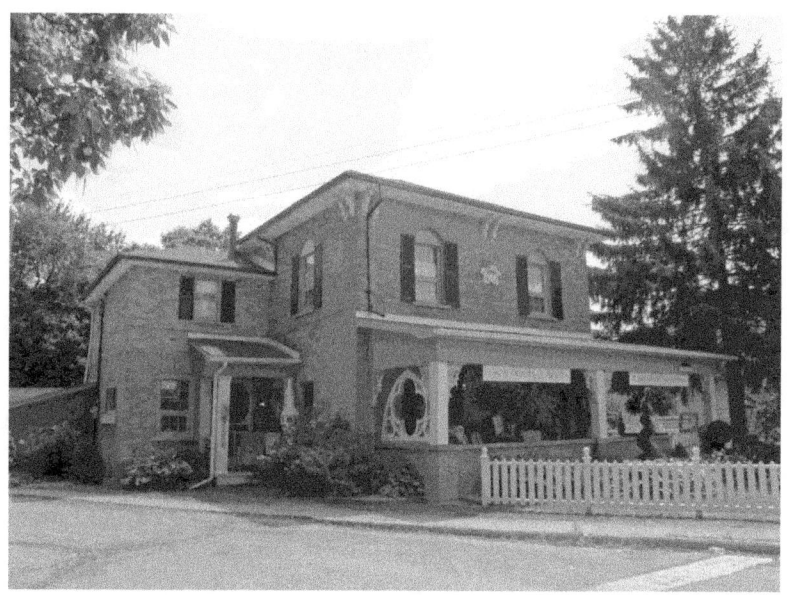

Italianate style

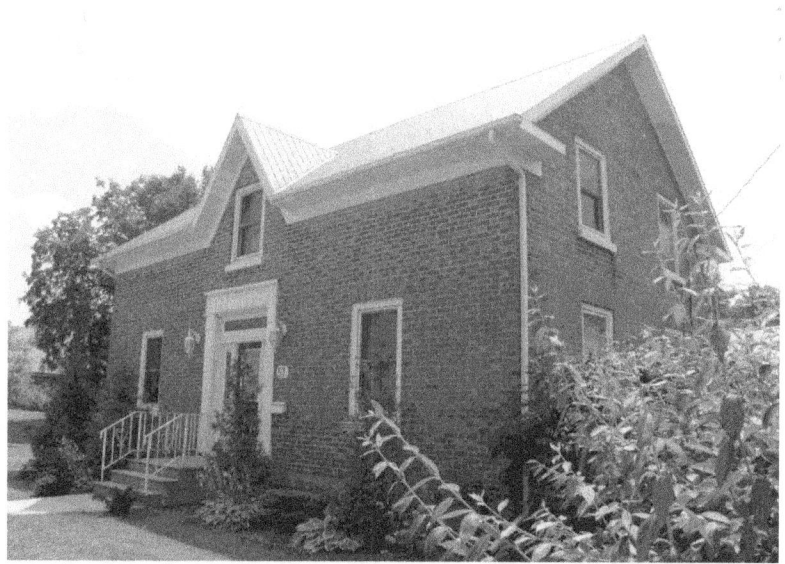

57 Talbot Street – 1½ storey Gothic Revival cottage, cornice return on end gable, red brick

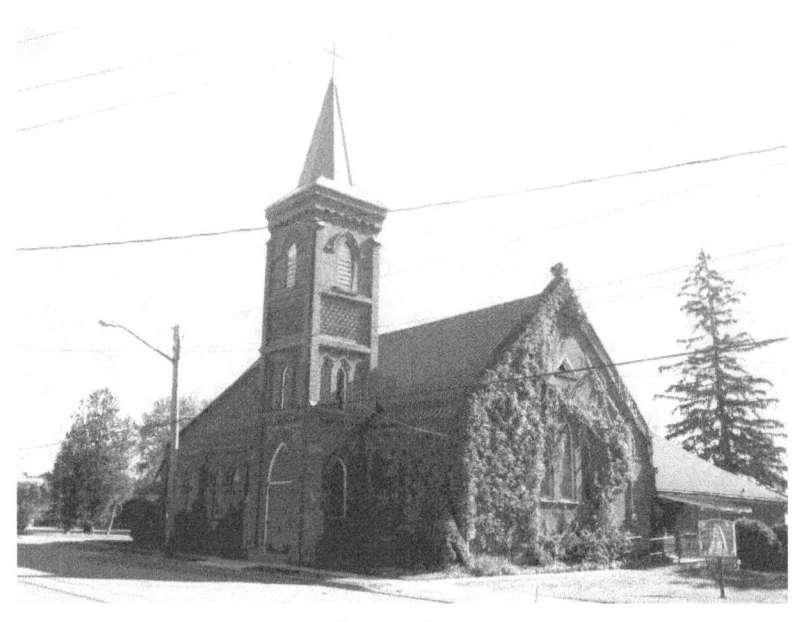

St. Paul's Anglican Church – 65 Talbot Street East

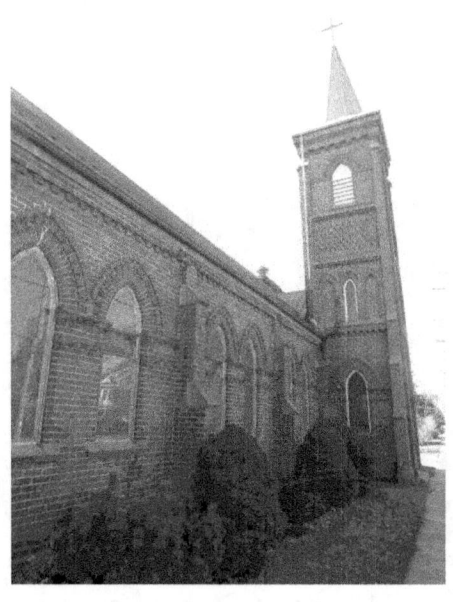

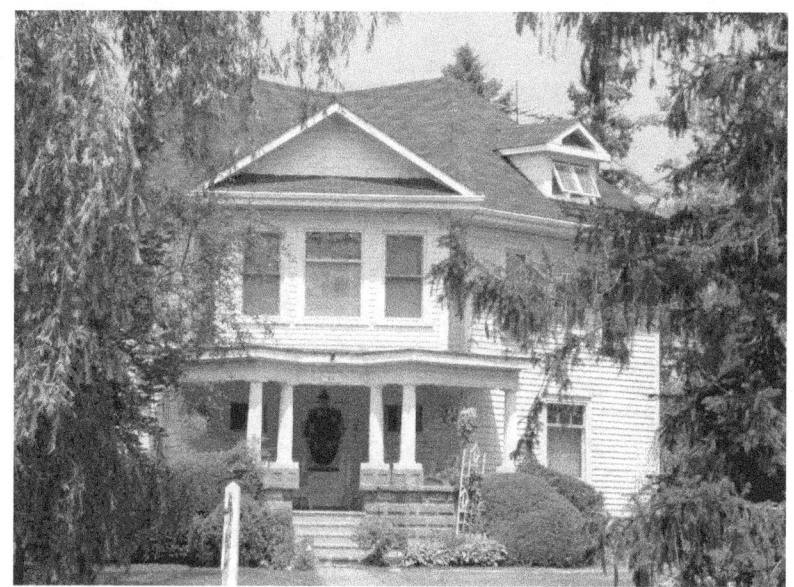

60 Talbot Street East – Italianate style with frontispiece, triangular pediment, dormer in the attic

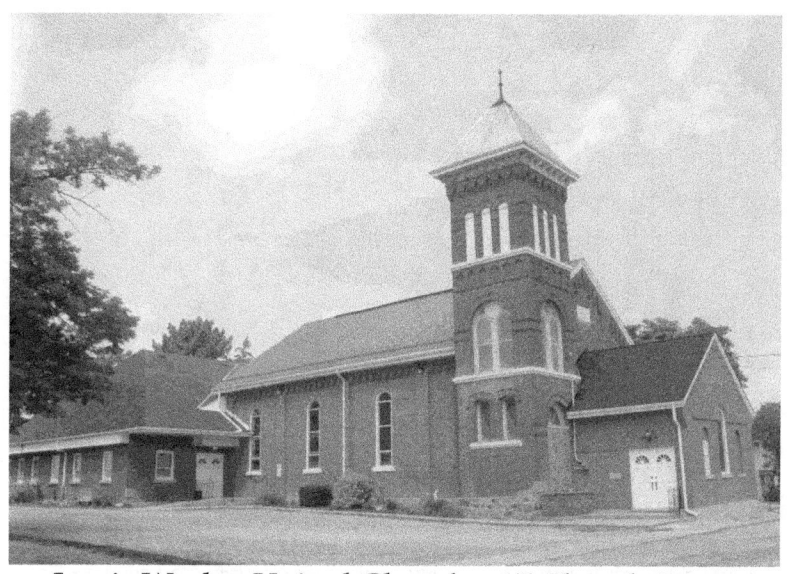

Jarvis Wesley United Church – 17 Church Street

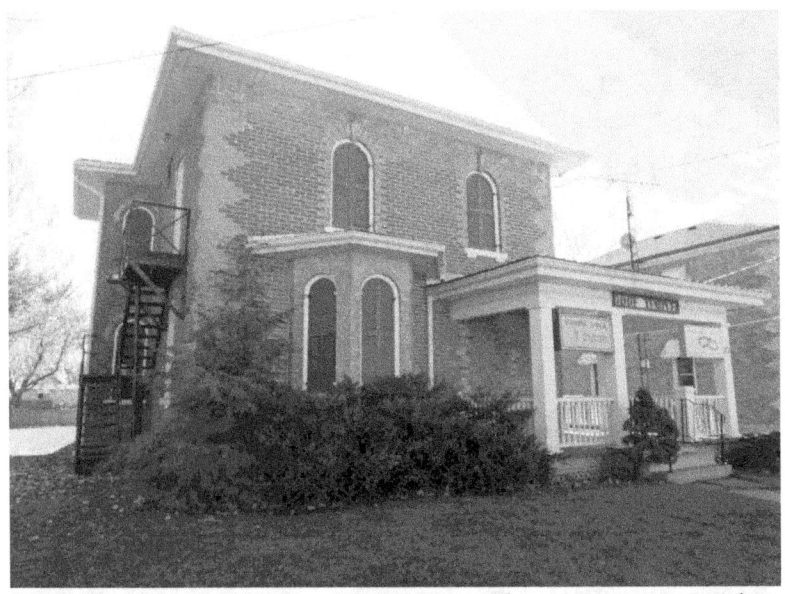

23 Talbot Street East – IOOF Temple – Masonic Lodge
Italianate style, dichromatic brickwork, bay window,
keystones above windows

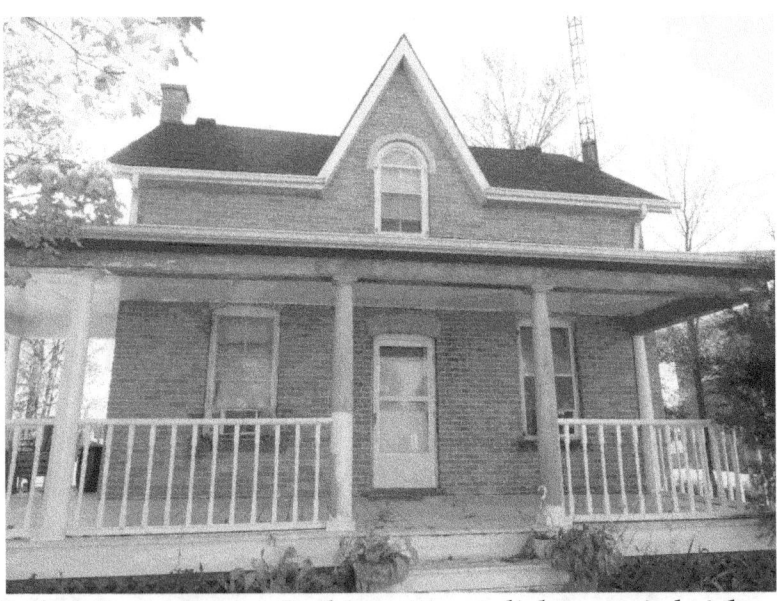

25 Talbot Street East – Gothic cottage, dichromatic brickwork,
buff-coloured window hoods

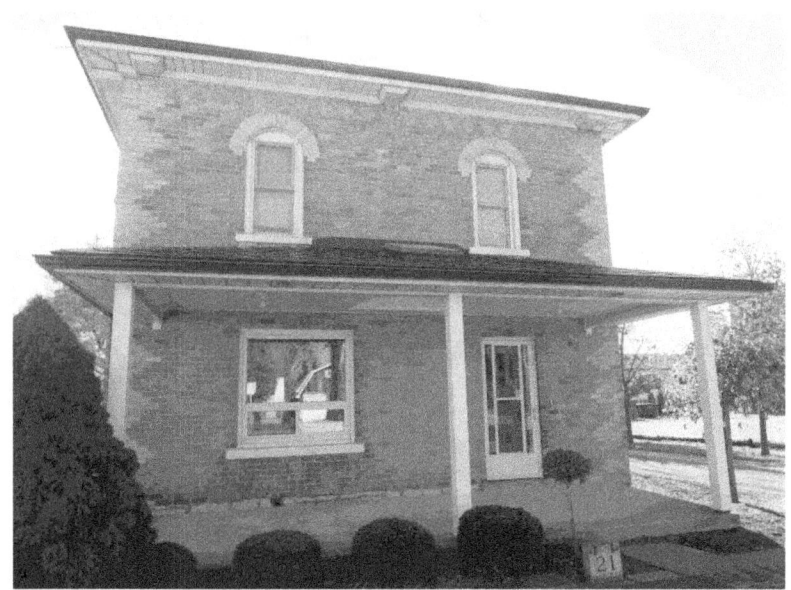

21 Talbot Street – Italianate style, arched window hoods

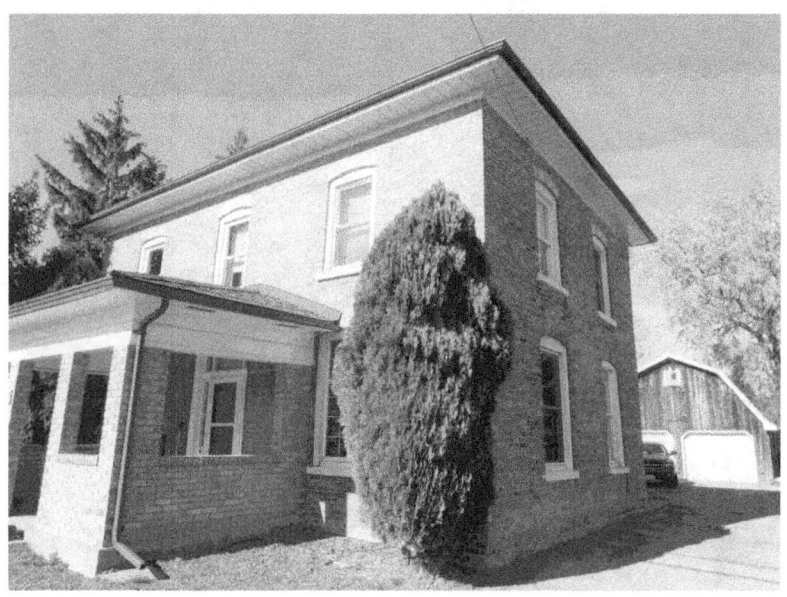

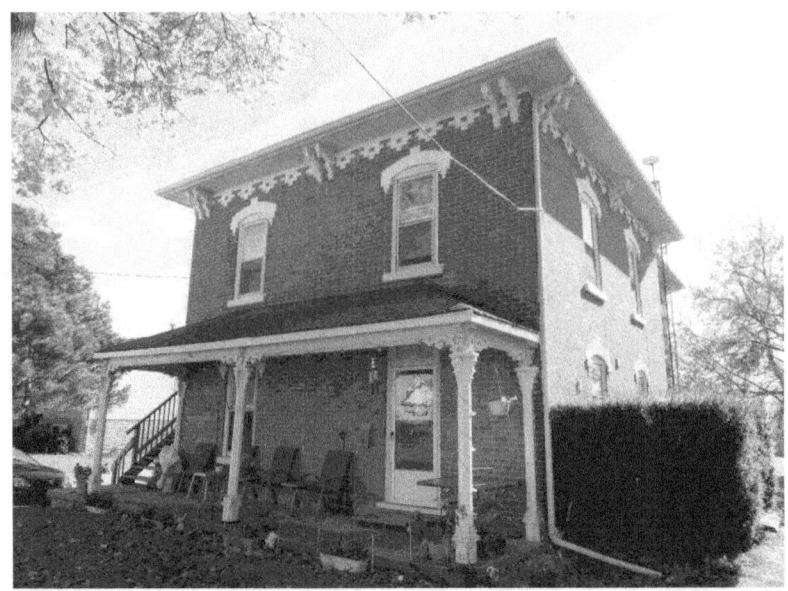

53 Talbot Street – Italianate style, paired cornice brackets, dichromatic patterning below cornice, arched window hoods

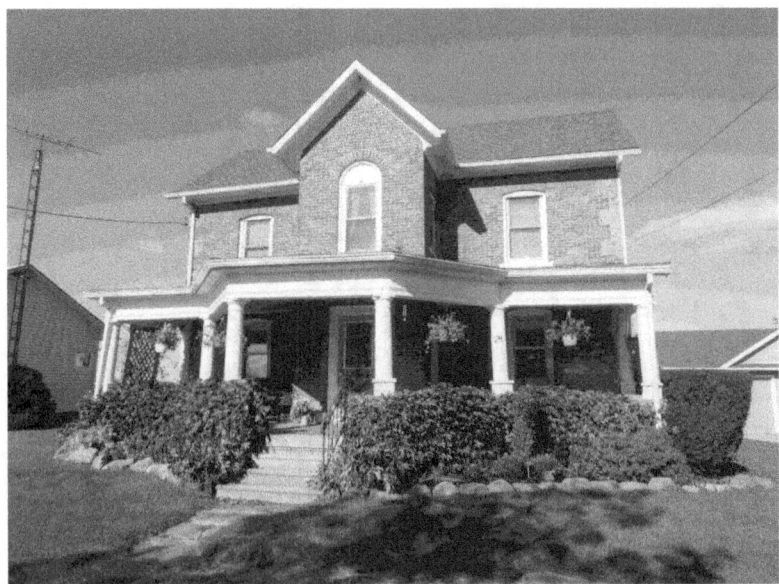

24 Talbot Street – Gothic Revival style – red brick, corner quoins

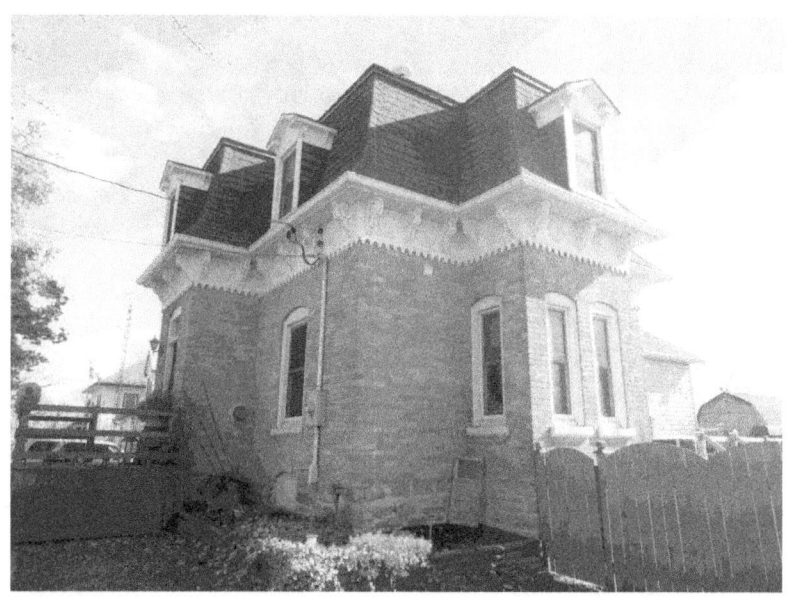

45 Talbot Street – Second Empire style – mansard roof, dormers in roof, single cornice brackets, cornice return on small window gables

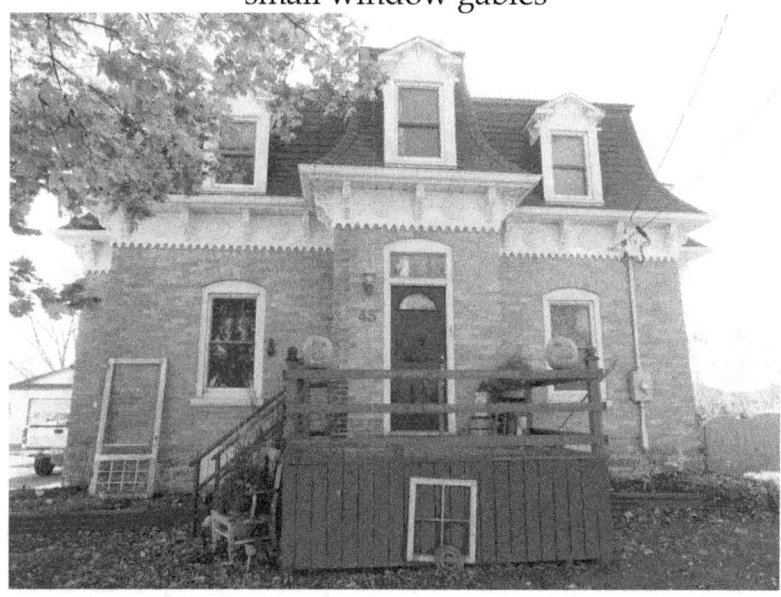

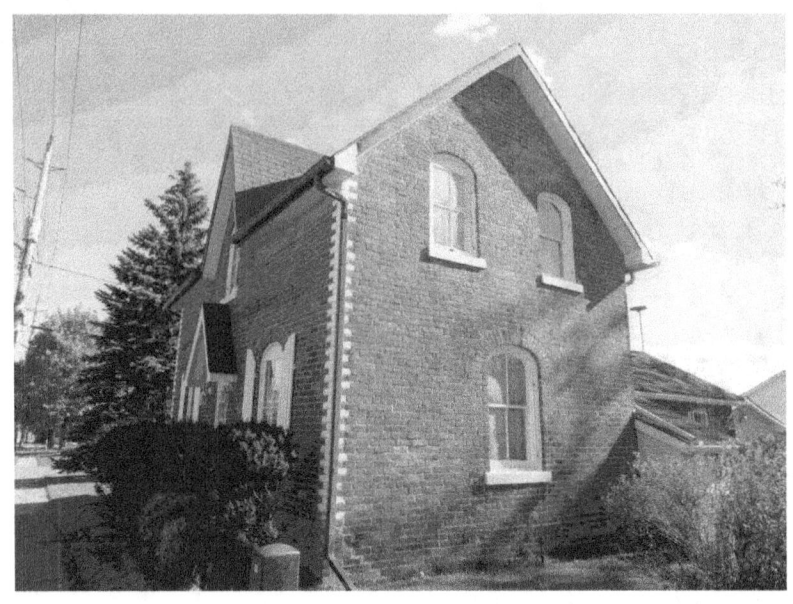

#31 – Gothic Revival – 1½ storeys, arched voussoirs

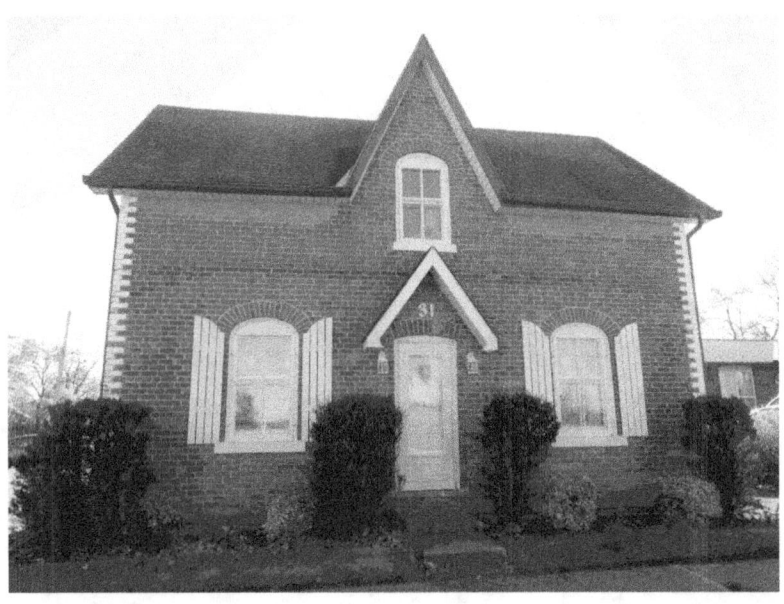

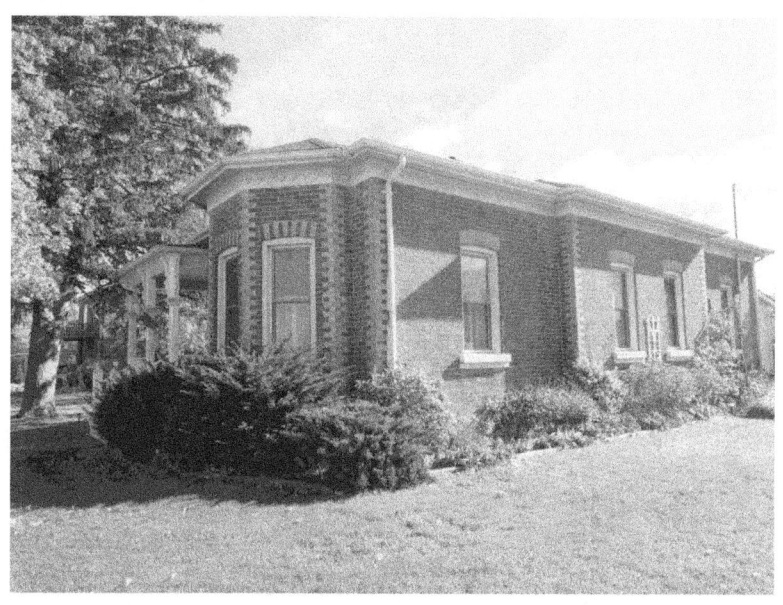

25 Talbot Street – dichromatic brickwork, corner quoins – Italianate style – unusual one floor only

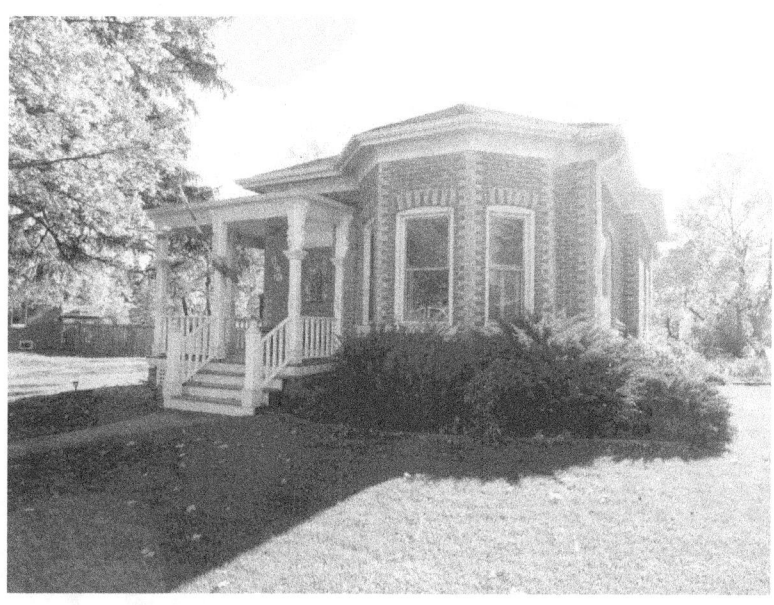

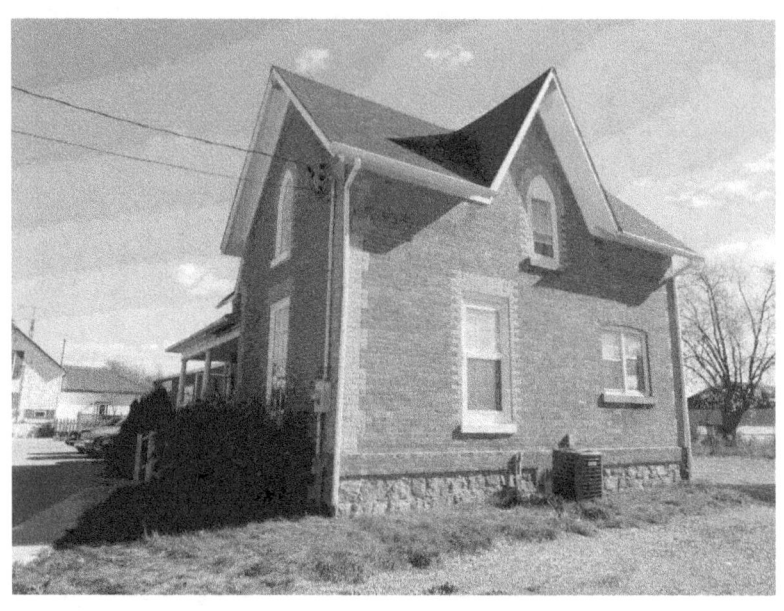

Gothic Revival style – dichromatic brickwork

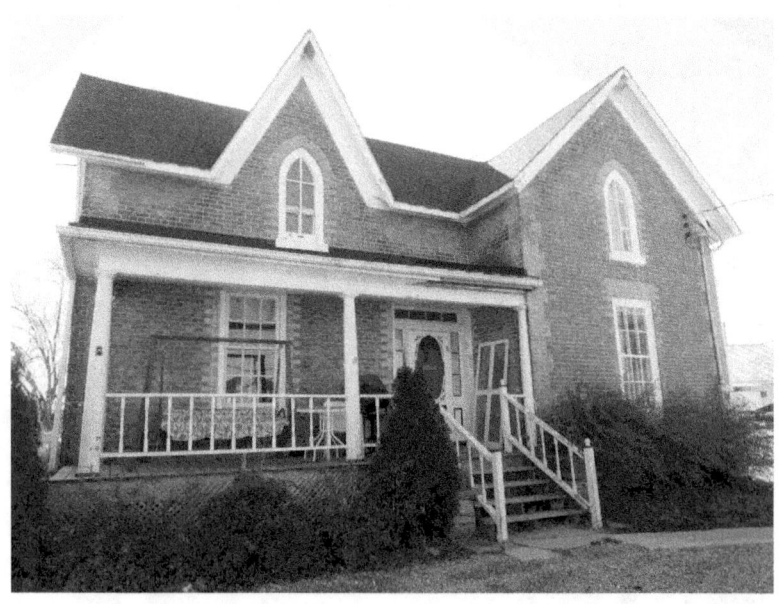

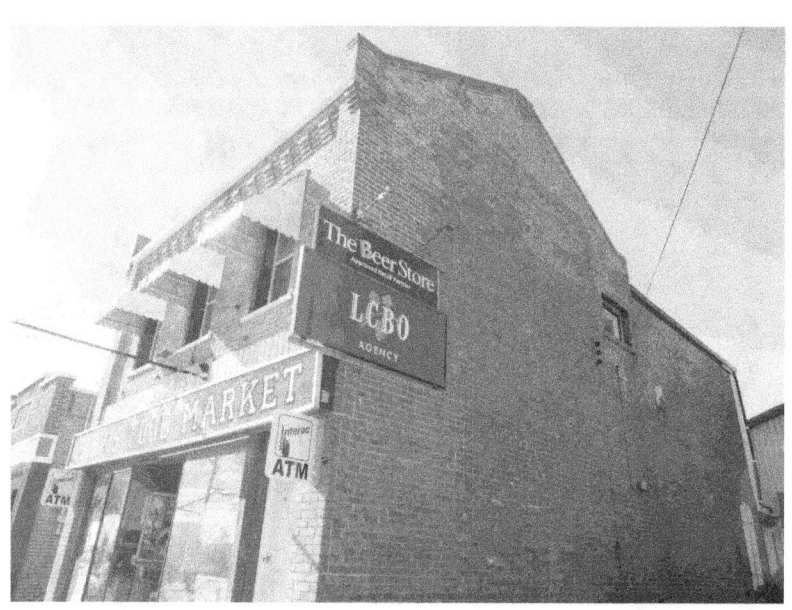

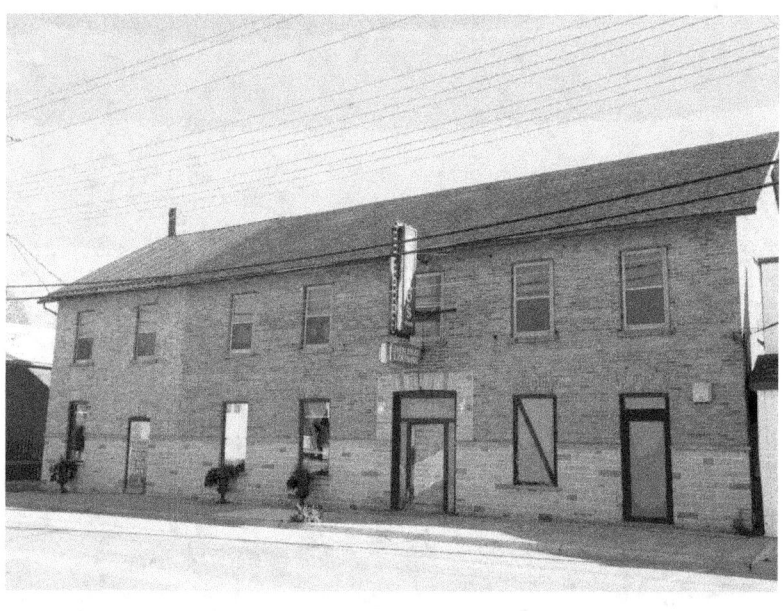

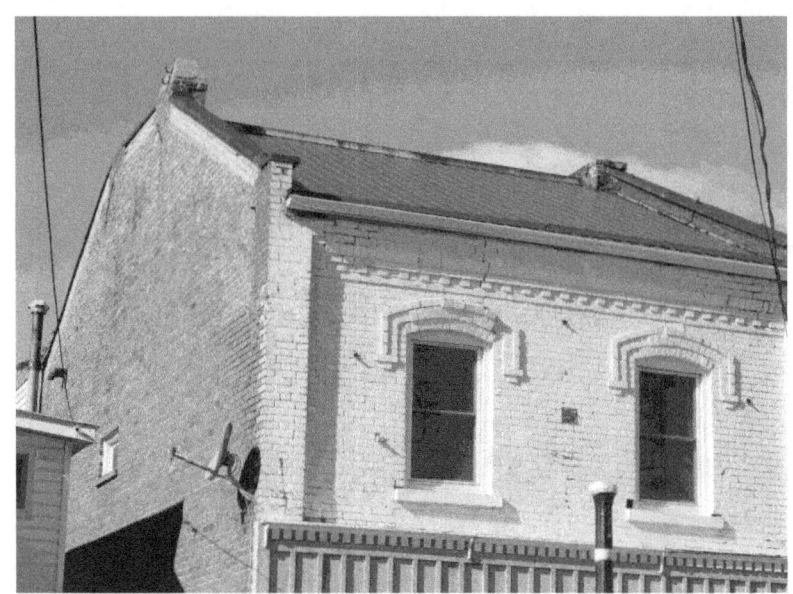
Fancy window voussoirs

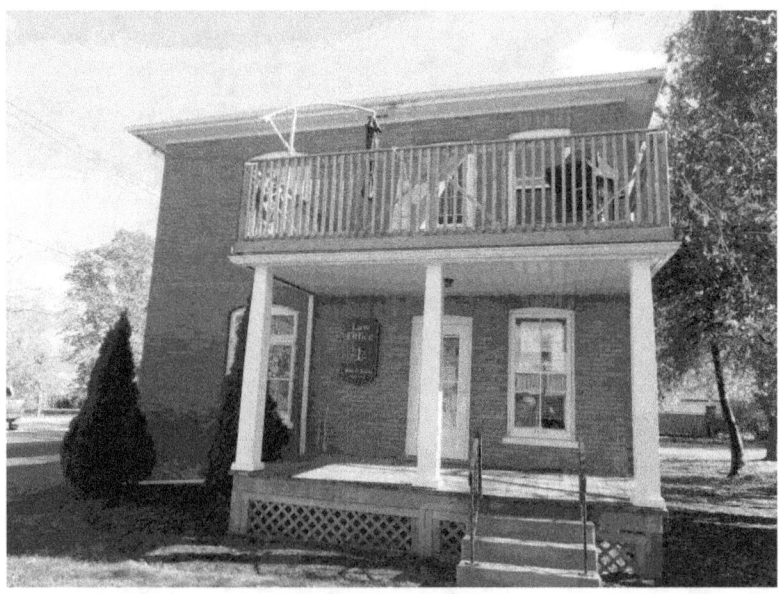
Italianate style

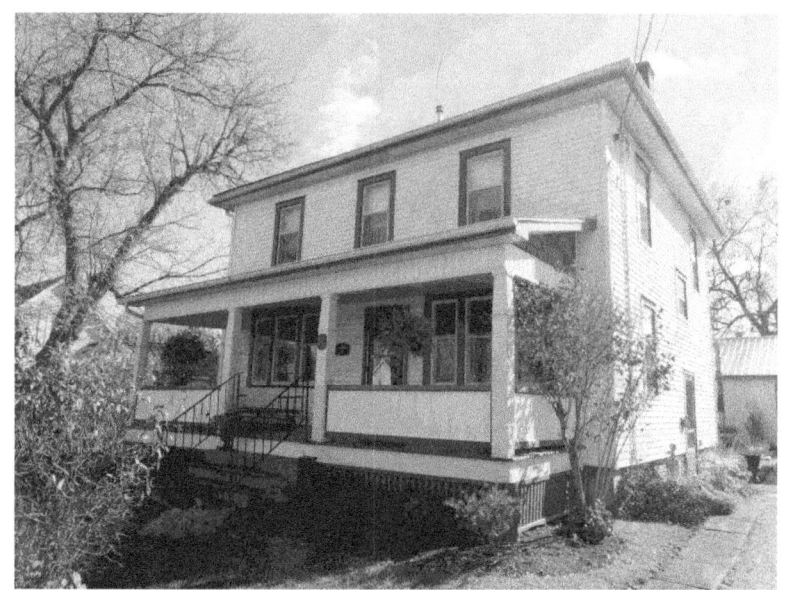

#8 – Italianate style – upgraded with siding

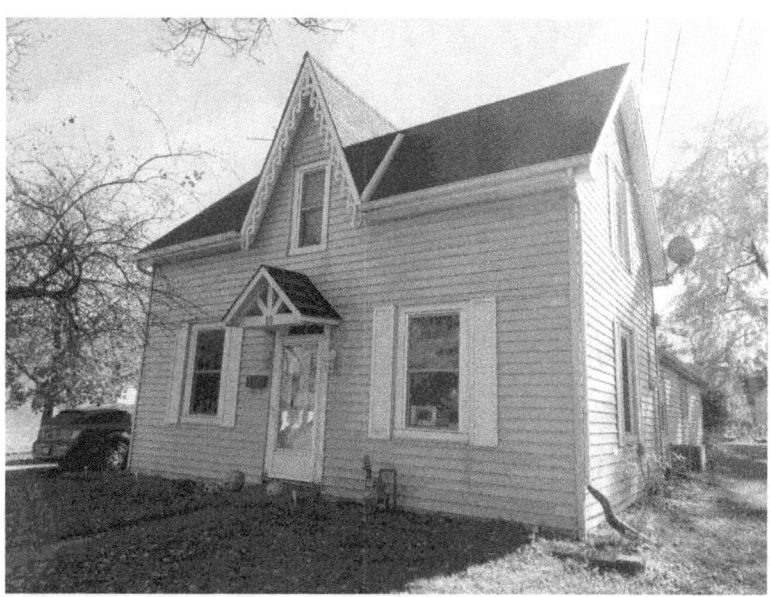

#10 - Gothic Revival with Vergeboard trim on the attic gable

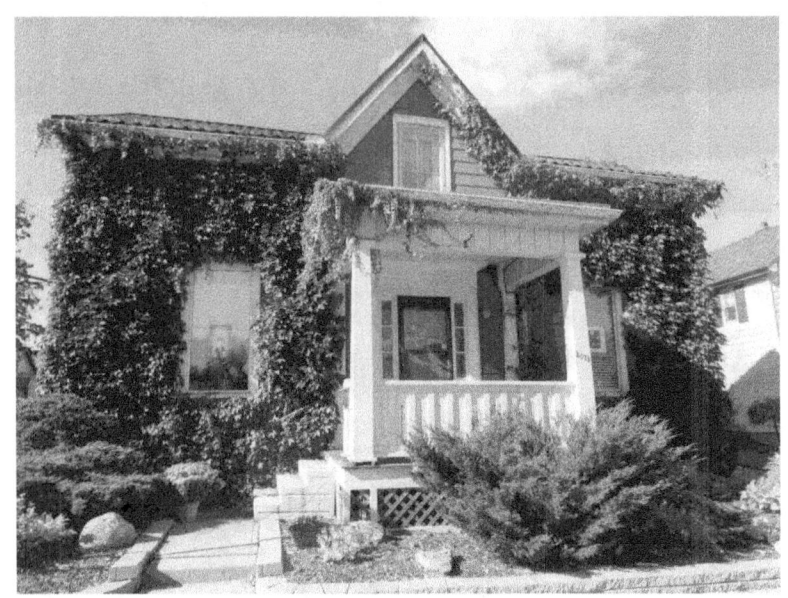

2033 Main Street

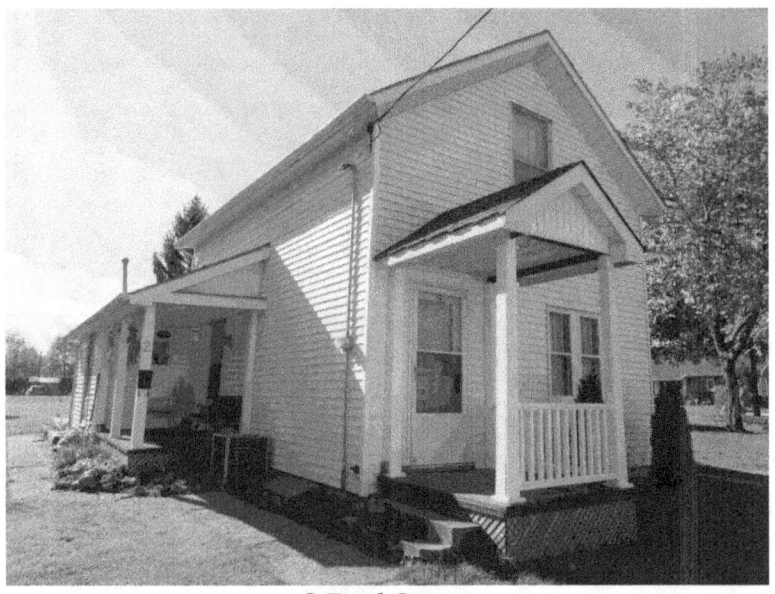

2 Peel Street

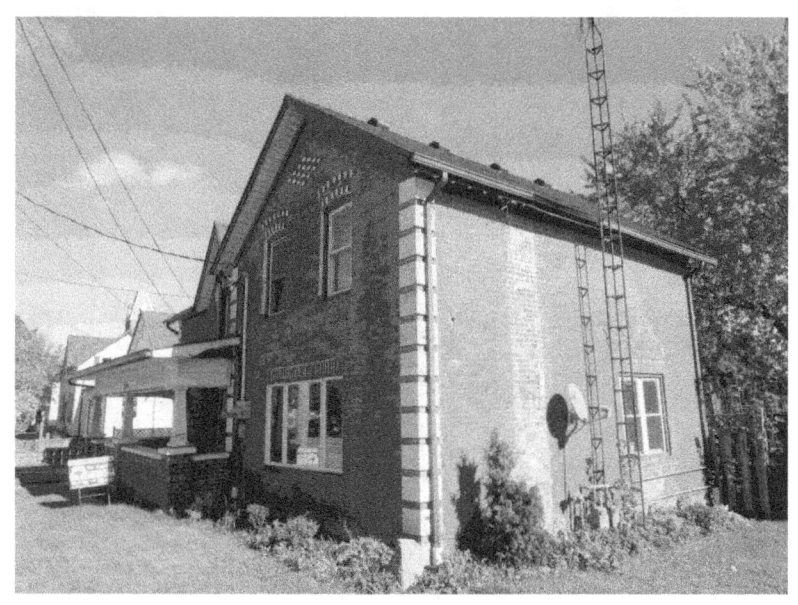

2046 Main Street

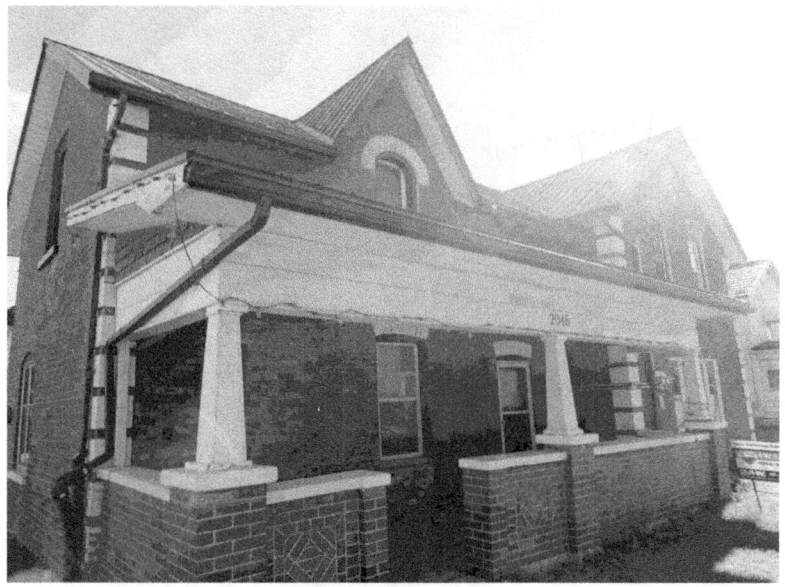

Gothic Revival

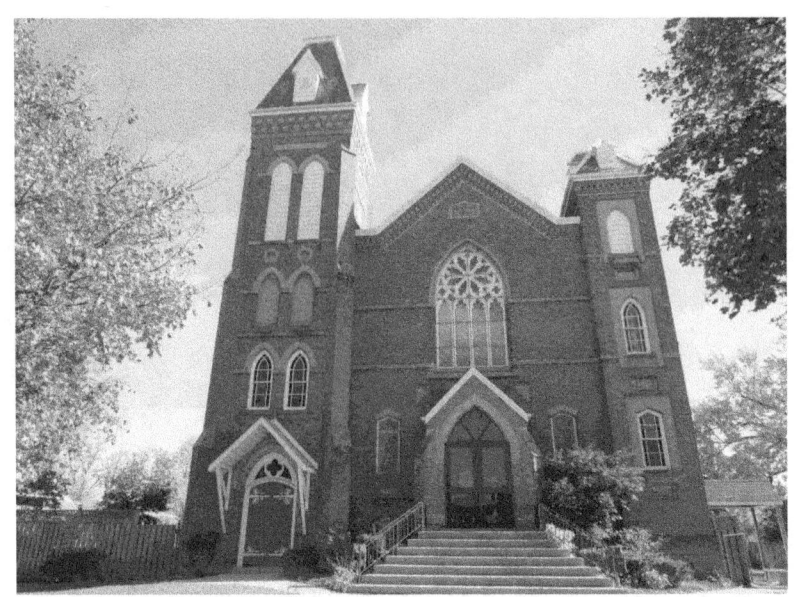

Knox Church – 1896 – dichromatic banding and brickwork, dichromatic tile work in tower

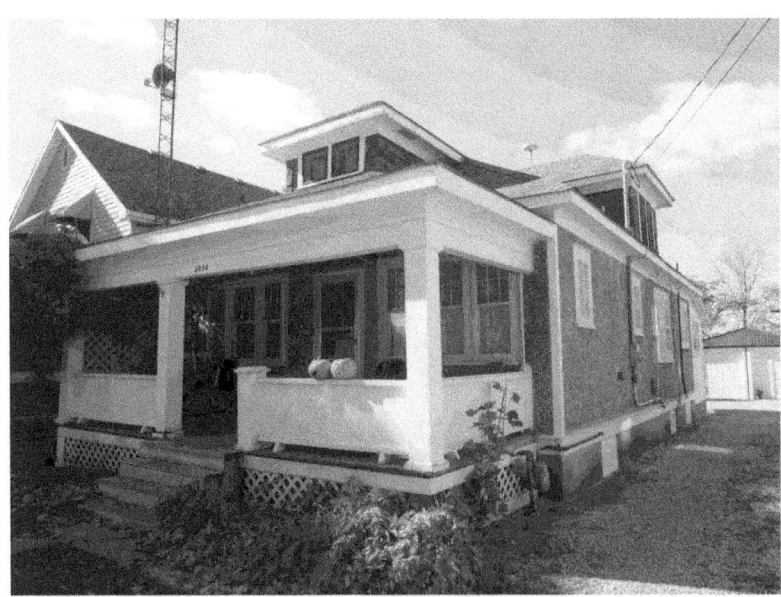

2055 Main Street – Italianate – dormer in roof – stucco exterior

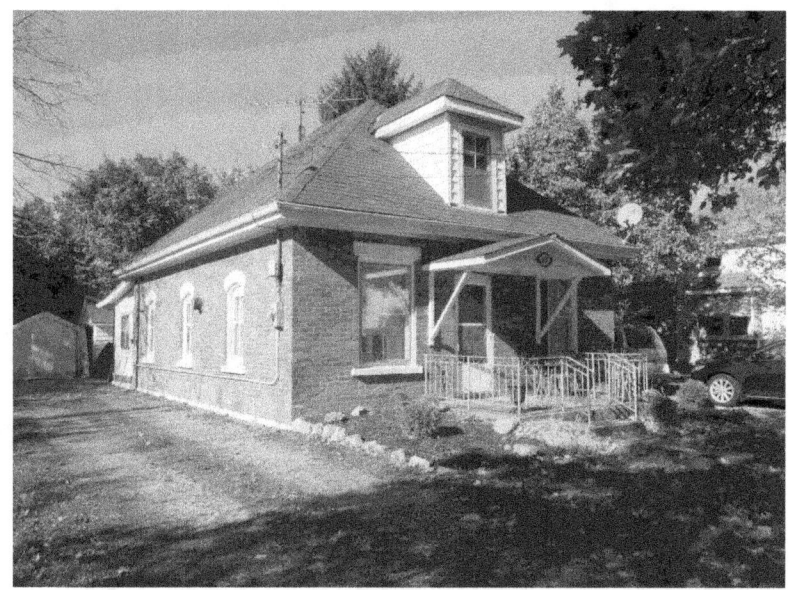

2051 Main Street – excellent example of a dormer in the hip roof – Italianate style

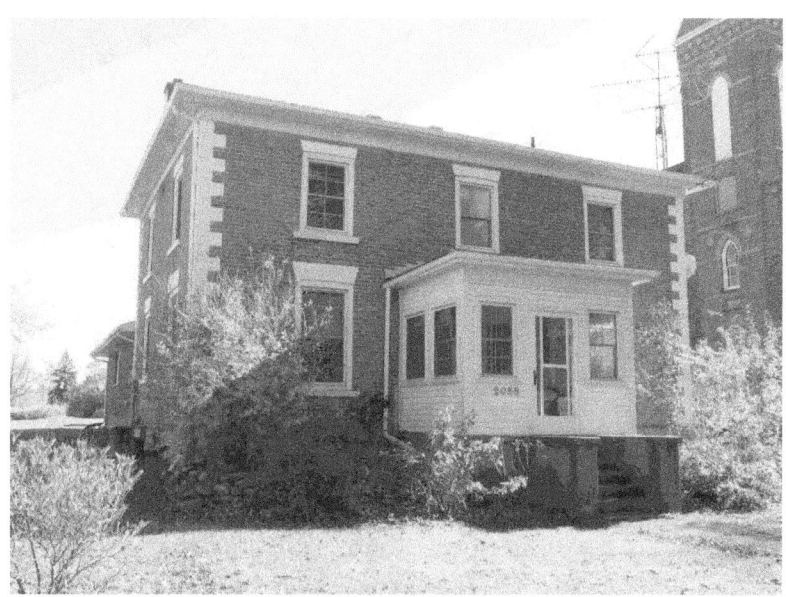

2058 Main Street – Italianate style, dichromatic brickwork

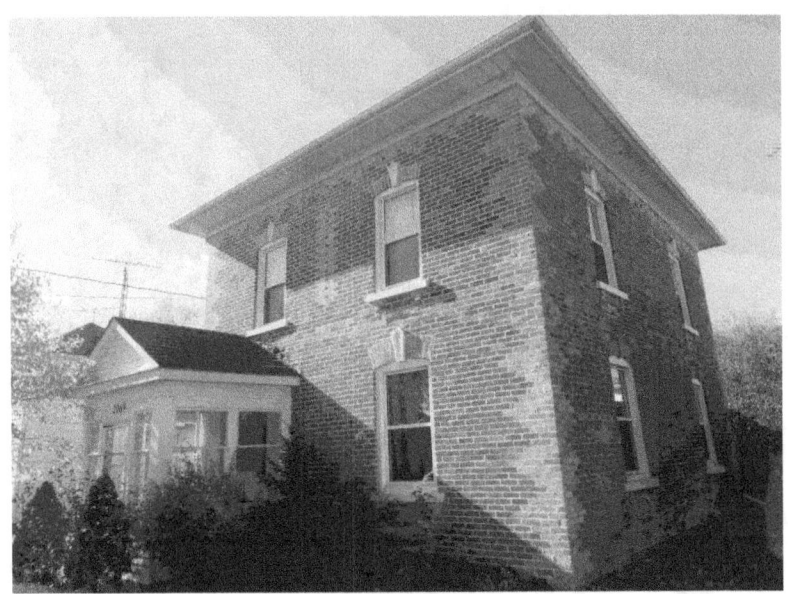

2069 Main Street – Italianate, dichromatic brickwork, voussoirs with keystones

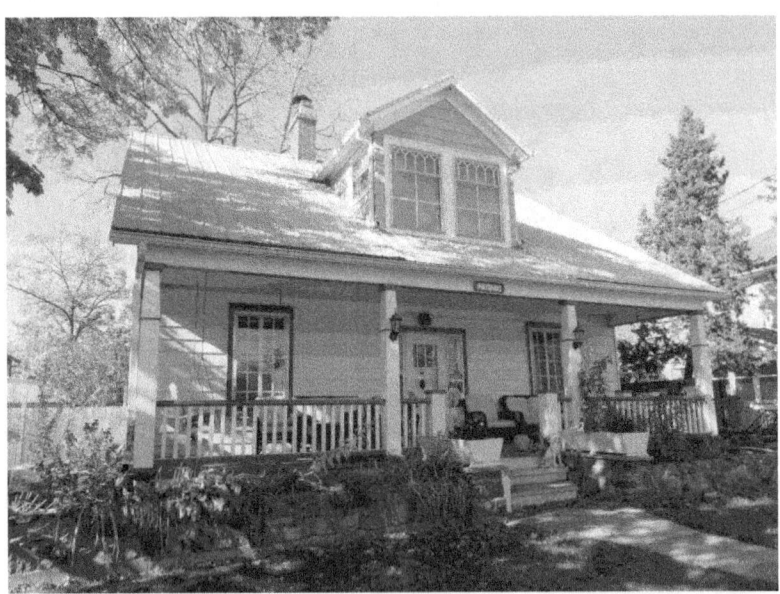

2073 Main Street – dormer in attic – Gothic cottage

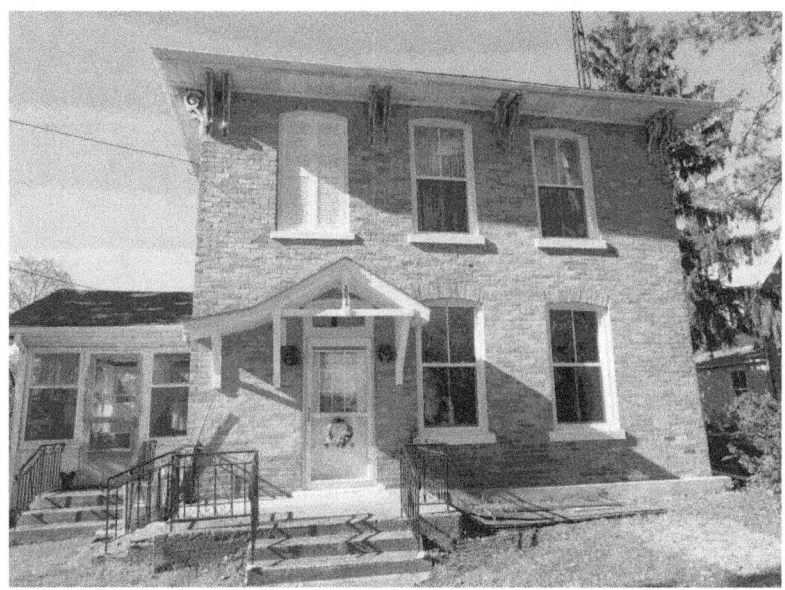

2075 Main Street – Italianate style with paired cornice brackets

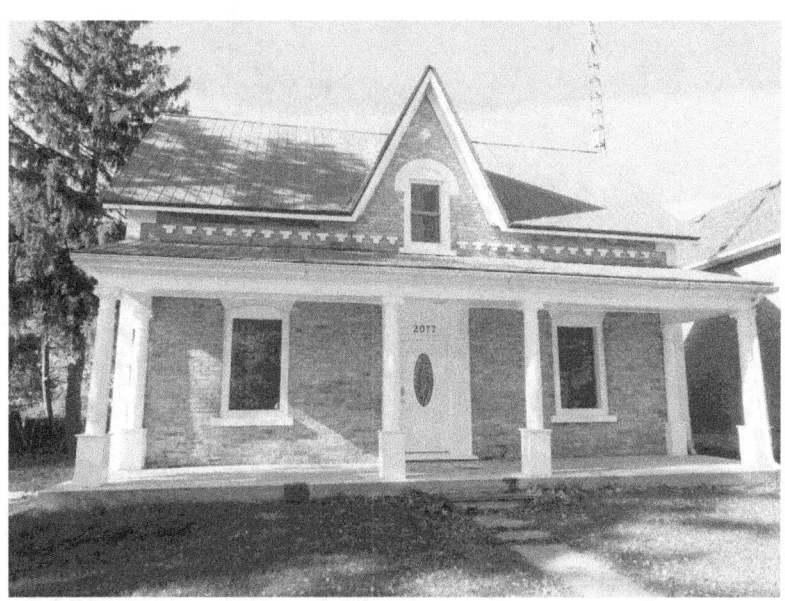

2077 Main Street – arched window hood in attic gable – Gothic cottage, light red brick, decorative brickwork below cornice

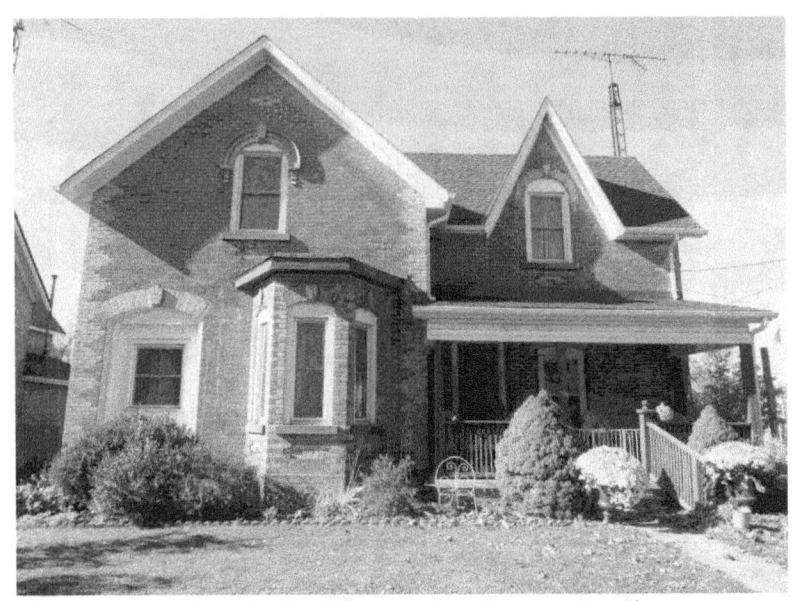

2079 Main Street - Gothic Revival – decorative keystones and voussoirs, bay window, dichromatic brickwork

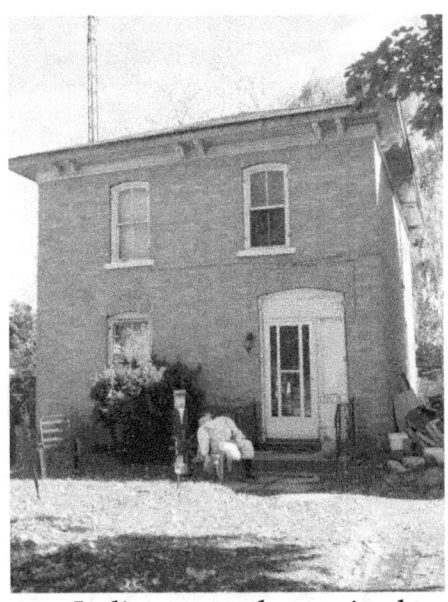

2080 Main Street – Italianate style – paired cornice brackets, orange/red brick

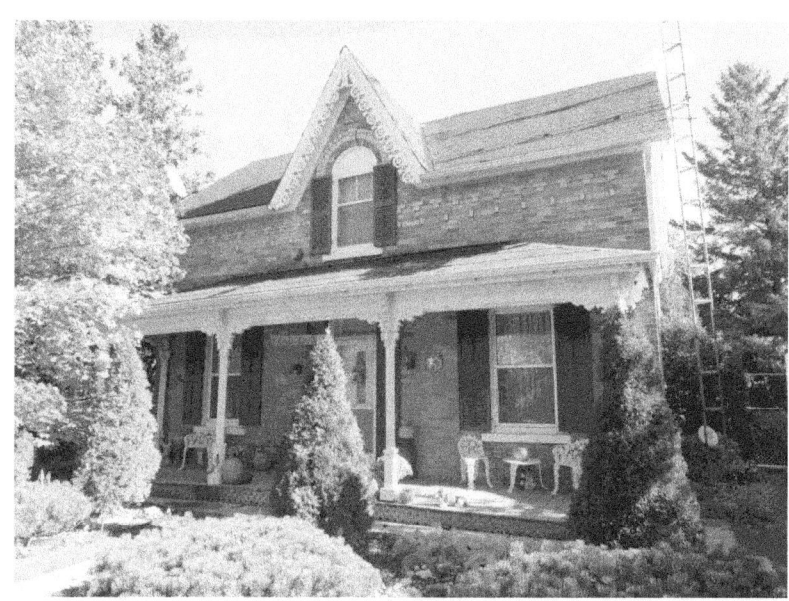

Gothic Revival – Vergeboard trim on gable, arched voussoirs and keystones, orange/red brick, decorative brickwork below cornice – "Meadwood"

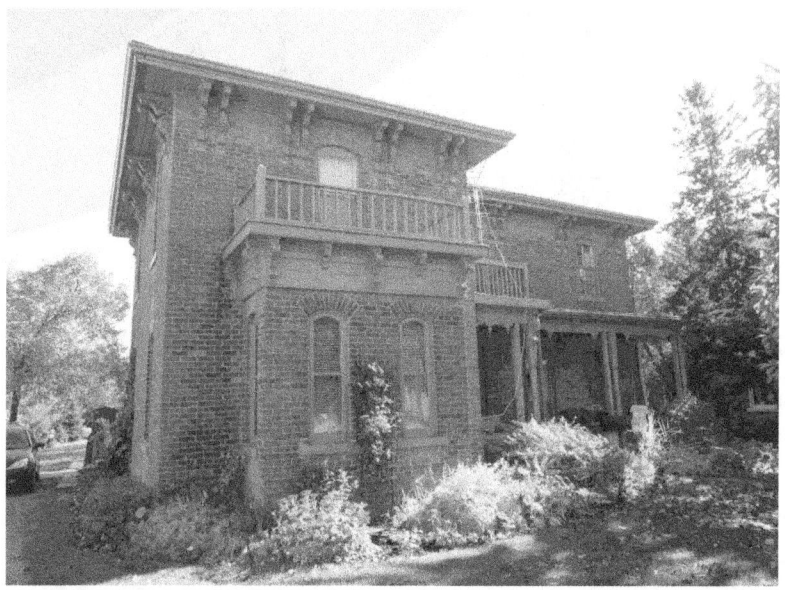

2086 Main Street – Italianate – paired cornice brackets, arched voussoirs, red brick

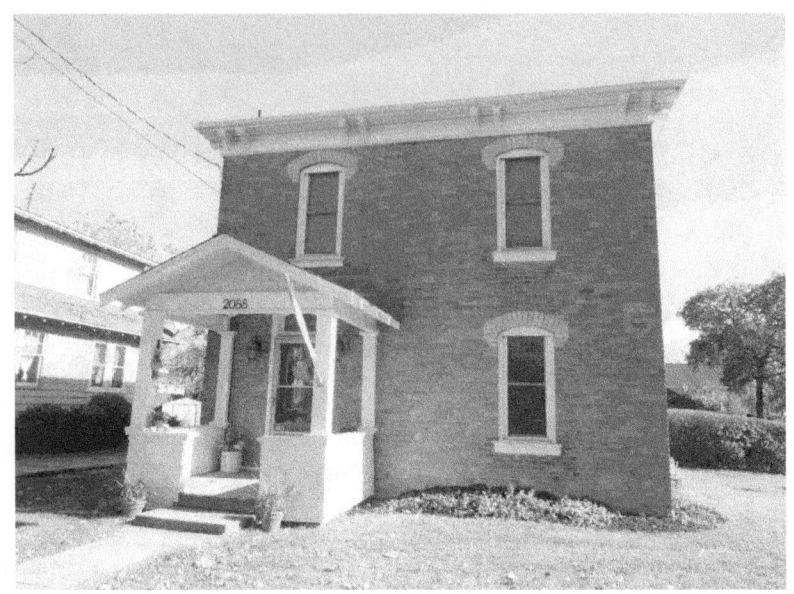

2088 Main Street – two storey, Italianate, arched window hoods, paired cornice brackets

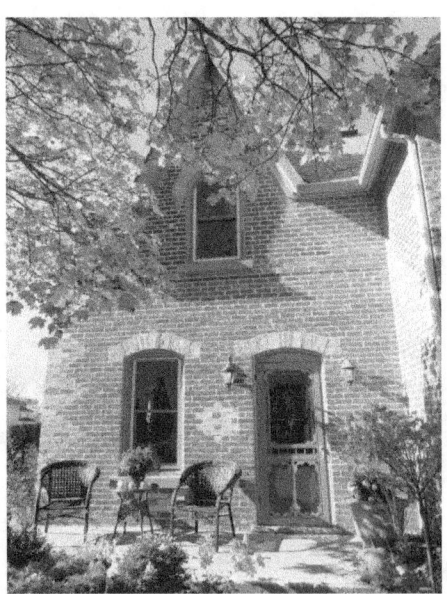

Gothic Revival – dichromatic brickwork

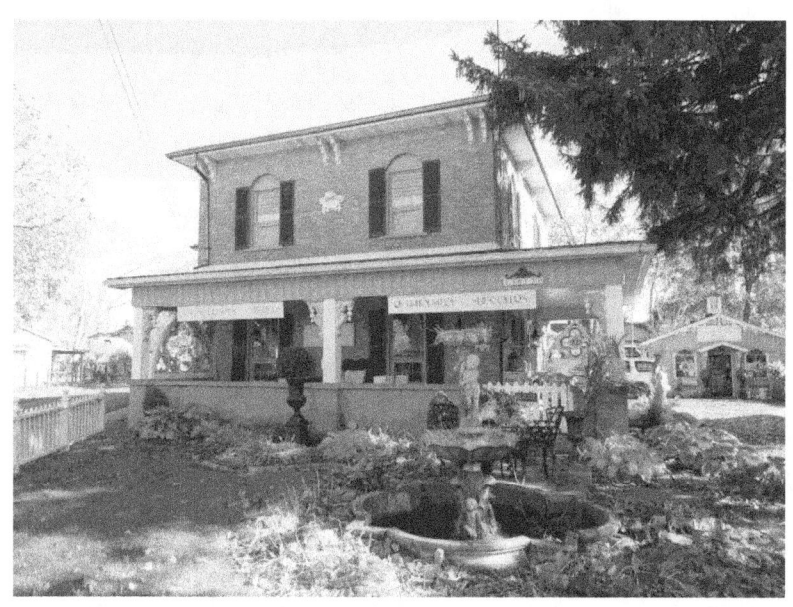

2092 Main Street – Italianate – c. 1870

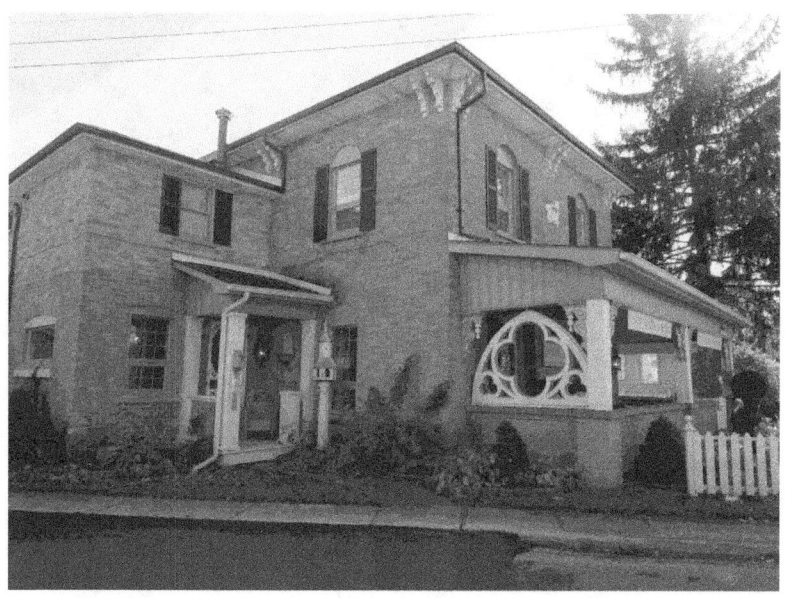

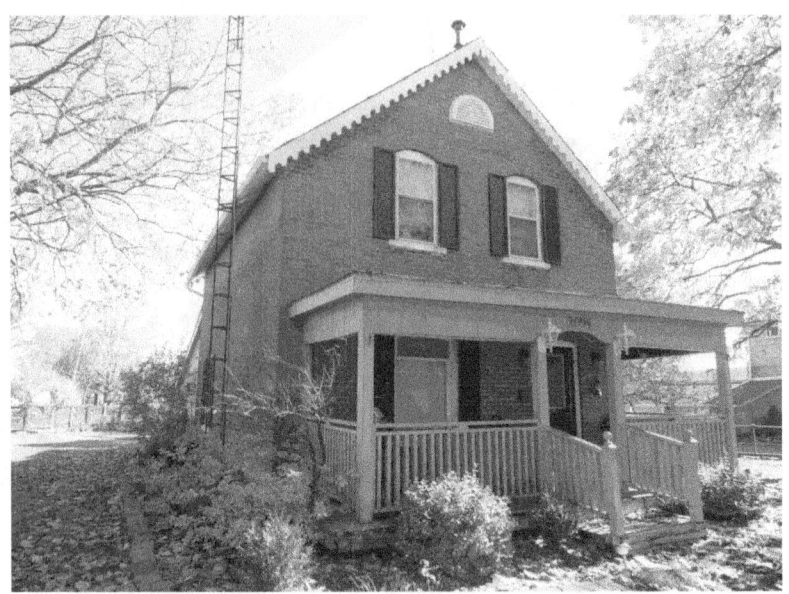

2094 Main Street – Vergeboard trim on gable

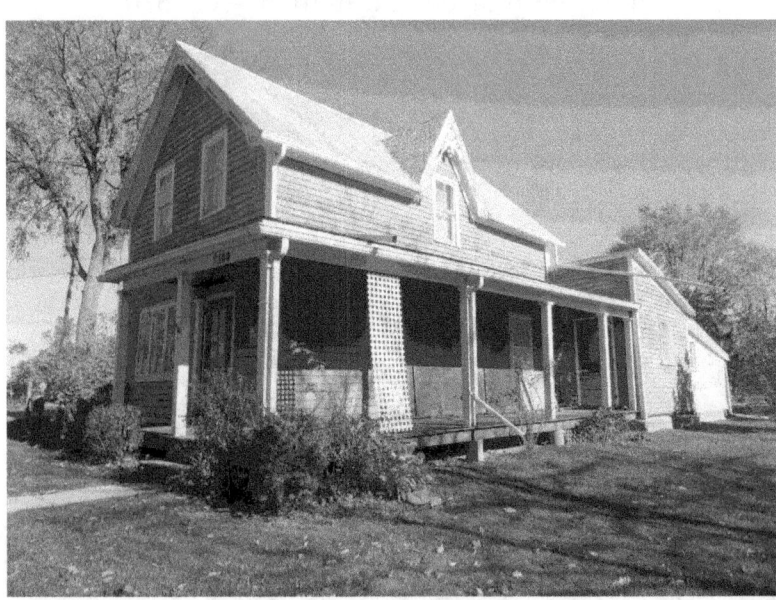

2100 Main Street – Gothic Revival – wood siding – Vergeboard trim on gables

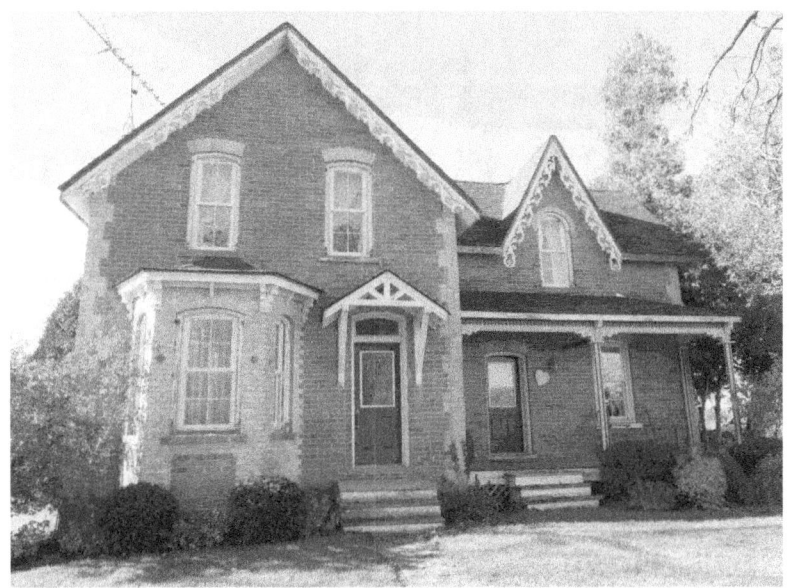

2145 Main Street - Gothic Revival – Vergeboard trim, bay window with cornice brackets

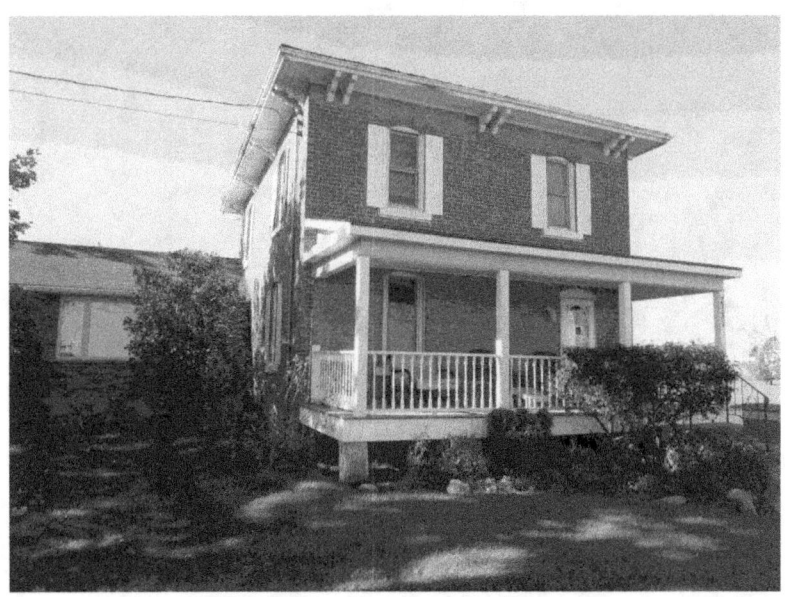

2137 Main Street – Italianate

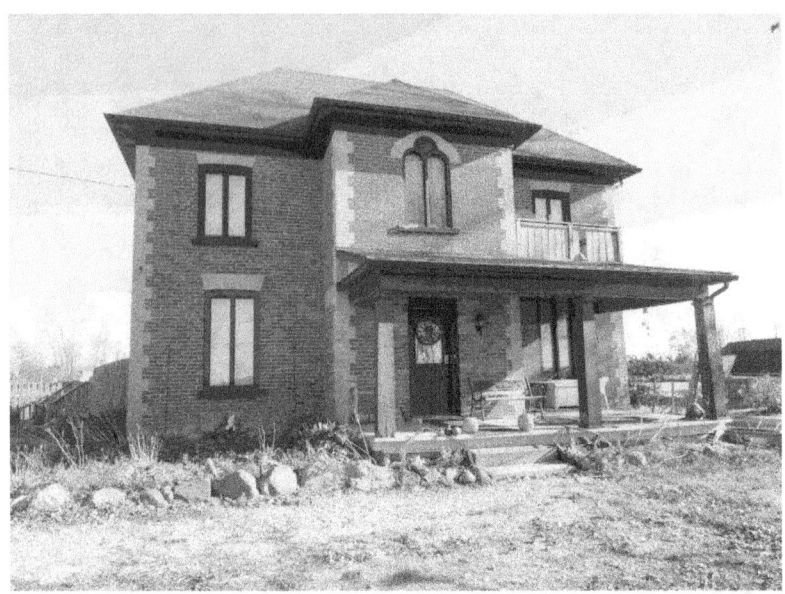

c. 1847 – Italianate, hipped roof, dichromatic brickwork

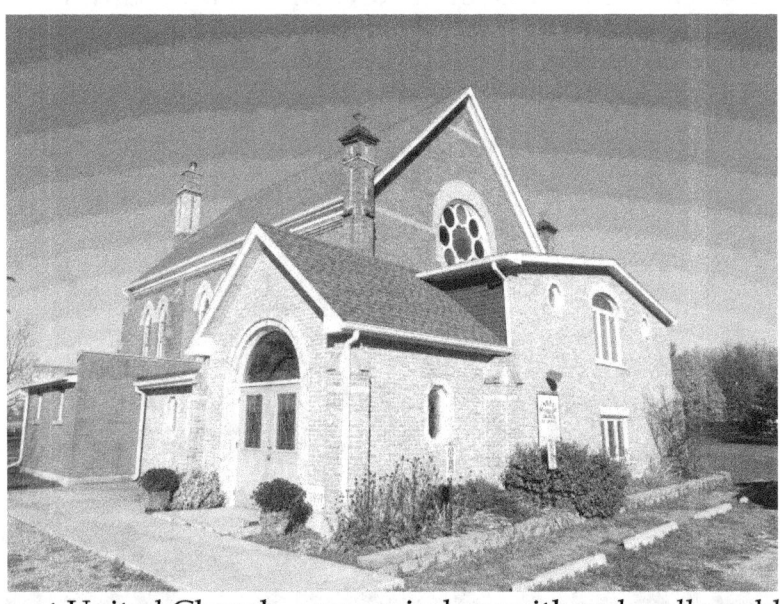

Garnet United Church – rose window with red, yellow, blue, green, navy, and magenta circles – back portion c. 1889 (Methodist Church), front addition 1997

Architectural Terms

Brackets: a decorative or weight-bearing structural element which forms a right angle with one side against a wall and the other under a projecting surface such as an eave or roof. Example: 2075 Main Street, Jarvis	
Cobblestone architecture: Refers to the use of cobblestones embedded in mortar as a method for erecting walls on houses and commercial buildings. Example: Wesley United Church	
Cornice: originally the wooden overhang of the roof. With the use of stone, brick, iron and steel, the cornice is any projecting shelf at the top of a ceiling or roof. They can be very decorative. Example:	
Cornice Return: decorative element on the end of a gable. Example: 45 Talbot Street	
Dentil Moulding: an even series of rectangles used as ornamental decoration in cornices. Example: Knox Church	
Dichromatic brickwork: the use of two colours of brick, tile or slate to decorate a façade. Example: 53 Talbot Street	
Dormer: (French for "sleep") a gable end window that pierces through the plane of a sloping roof surface to create usable space in the top floor or attic of a building by adding headroom. Example: 2150 Main Street, Jarvis	

Gable: the triangular portion of a wall between the edges of a sloping roof. Example: 2094 Main Street	
Hipped Roof: a roof where all sides slope downwards to the walls with no gables.	
Keystones and Voussoirs: a voussoir is a wedge-shaped element used in building an arch. A keystone is the central stone that locks all the stones into position, allowing the arch to bear weight. A keystone is often enlarged and embellished. Example: 2079 Main Street	
Lancet Window: a tall, narrow window with a pointed arch at its top. Example: Knox Church, Jarvis	
Mansard Roof: This style was popularized by Francois Mansart (1598-1666), an accomplished architect of the French Baroque period and especially fashionable during the Second French Empire (1852-1870). This roof is almost flat on the top section, with two slopes on each of its sides with the lower slope at a steeper angle than the upper and having dormer windows. Example: 45 Talbot Street, Jarvis	

Pediment: a triangular section above the horizontal structure (entablature), typically supported by columns. The inside of the triangle is called the tympanum. Example: 60 Talbot Street East	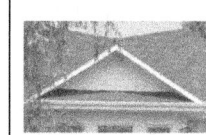
Quoin: masonry blocks at the corner of a wall, often a decorative feature, usually larger or of a different colour than the rest of the wall. Example:	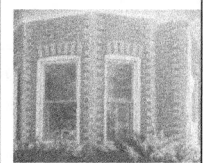
Rose Window: a circular window with ornamental tracery radiating from the centre. Example: Knox Church, Jarvis	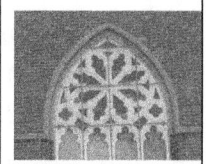
Vergeboard and Finial: also called bargeboards – hang from the projecting end of a roof and are often elaborately carved and ornamented. **Finial:** ornament added to the top of a gable, pinnacle, canopy or spire – a Gothic element.	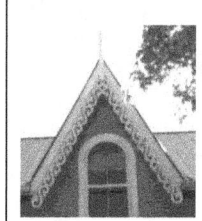
Window Hood: A **hood** is the piece found above window openings, usually of an ornate design, and covers the top third of the opening. Hoods are commonly placed above arched or curved openings on both windows and doors. Example: 21 Talbot Street	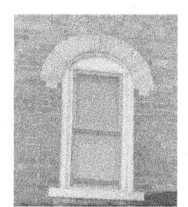

Jarvis' Building Styles

Gothic Revival, 1830-1890 – These decorative buildings have sharply-pitched gables with highly detailed vergeboards, pointed-arch window openings, and dichromatic brickwork. It is a common style in Ontario. Example: 2145 Main Street	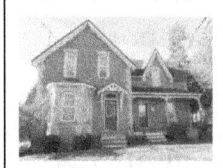
Italianate, 1850-1900 – It has wide-bracketed eaves, belvederes, wrap-around verandahs. Example: 2086 Main Street	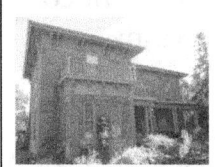
Second Empire, 1860-1880 – The mansard roof is the most noteworthy feature of this style and is evidence of the French origins. Projecting central towers and one or two-storey bays can also be present. Example: 45 Talbot Street	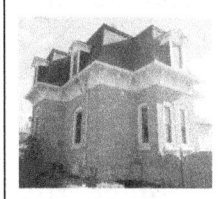

www.ingramcontent.com/pod-product-compliance
Lightning Source LLC
Chambersburg PA
CBHW070726180526
45167CB00004B/1636